HUNGRY for GHOSTS

Kristin's words of love and loss reflect the bittersweet touch of the ghosts that linger.
—KG Carroll
Poet & Author

Kristin Kory's poems feel like a walk on a moonlit night. They are hauntingly beautiful, visceral, and achingly transcendent.
—Trisha Leigh Shufelt
Author of The Ghosts of Winterbourne

Within these pages are words so beautifully haunting that your only desire is to turn to the next page. Kristin's heart and soul are poured on to the pages of this book.
—Charlene Fox
Author of Acceptance

When the night played its tune and ghosts of the forsaken suffered its consequences, that is how Kristin's brilliance was born.
—S.A. Quinox
Author of Tales of Lacrimosa

REVISED SECOND EDITION

HUNGRY *for* GHOSTS

POETRY
BY

KRISTIN KORY

300 SOUTH MEDIA GROUP
NEW YORK

HUNGRY FOR GHOSTS
SECOND EDITION

ISBN-13: 978-1-957596-17-4 (paperback)
ISBN-13: 978-1-957596-18-1 (ebook)

Cover & Interior Design by Indie Author Solutions
Published by 300 South Media Group

To all the ghosts I've loved before:
this house is not your home.

TABLE OF CONTENTS

Author's Note
Hungry For Ghosts

AUTHOR'S NOTE

I learned at a young age to never stare into the darkness,
to look away before I longed to see a face.

They floated and flickered like old dreams.
Some of them felt like homesickness.
I watched them drift from room to room.

They are everywhere, all around.

Some ghosts we make, some we keep.
Sometimes we squeeze our eyes shut
and hope they go away.

Faint footsteps in corridors.
Low voices in empty rooms.
Omnipresent longing in a song.
They are always here.

I don't care for the heavy ones,
the way they hover and pin you down.
Maybe it's sleep paralysis,
maybe it's a ghost.

It's not easy to distinguish
memories from ghosts.
Sometimes they are both.

Some ghosts you must fight to find your way
back from, but first you need to figure out
which one is holding on.

You or the ghost

HUNGRY FOR GHOSTS

And when they ask,
tell them I left myself
like lonely souls do:
hungry for ghosts
with a heart
still full of you.

PART I

Despite it all,
love still lives here.

Hungry For Ghosts

I STILL WEEP FOR THE WRECKAGE, I CONFESS

Mother said to never
let passion leave without you,
but sometimes you don't notice
until it gets away from you,
until it's beyond the horizon,
where distance can only be
measured in misery.

I am half here, half there,
half alive, half dead
by the time I notice it's gone.

I am busy chasing ghosts
when it slips quietly out the door.
I am teetering between reality and dream.
I am mourning bones.

The thought of breaking free
from comfort's pillowy embrace
doesn't even cross my mind.

I am anchored here,
in the dark oblivion,
long past ruination.

Mother said to dwell here
long enough to make your peace,
but leave before the old pain
sings to you like a love song.

TOO LATE

I wanted to run,
but it was too late—
I had already fallen.
I was both
mesmerized
and terrified,
and I was losing control
in the most beautiful way.
I knew at that moment
that you'd be my undoing.
So, I thought
I should save myself,
I should run for the door,
but I didn't stand a chance
because all my pieces
were scattered across the floor,
and they looked so
terrifyingly helpless
as they whimpered,
I'm yours.

CRUSHED

You look at me and I look away
because my eyes can't keep a secret,
they'll tell you everything.

You sent me a song,
I made you a ghost.
Behind every smile,
there was a wish.
Between every nervous gulp,
I tried to catch my breath.
I loved in secret,
never breathing a word.
It crushed me so softly
and brutally, how badly
I could want someone
to haunt me.

UNDERSTAND

I wish I could
understand
what your eyes
are saying
because this
absence of words
is leaving
plenty of room
for my mind
to talk my heart
out of you.

TAKE ME

Take me there.
Tell me your dreams,
the ones you don't
speak of.
Show me what hides
in the shadows.
I don't care
how dark it is,
just take me
into your soul.

THE KNOWING

Beyond skin and bone,
without agenda,
without hope.

It's the way you look at me
and I unfold.
The way I look at you
and we both just know.

It's that unmistakable knowing,
deep down in our souls,
that we were never strangers,
we met some lifetimes ago.

DUST AND BONES

Of dust and bones
we make a home,
close to the heart
we've always known.

WE ARE NOT STRANGERS

We are not strangers,
we have already met.
We are two lost souls
who were lucky enough
to find each other again.

OLD FRIEND

It's good to see you, old friend.
I've missed your kind eyes,
I would recognize them anywhere,
and I haven't seen your sweet smile
since the last time our hearts danced.
Oh, what a precious gift it is,
when two souls find each other again.

GRAVEYARD

We made a graveyard
of the crumbled bits of nostalgia.
It was messy and littered
with sharp pieces and jagged edges.
But there was still plenty left
of the wreckage to be adored.

GEORGIE

Sometimes I think about
those cool July nights
when the humidity would break
and we'd walk around the city
for hours on end,
wandering the streets
littered with the noise of strangers,
always finding adventure,
often looking for danger.

I think back to that one night
when a June bug got caught in my hair,
and we both hated June bugs
so, we both just freaked out
until you eventually swatted it
out of my hair.

It's strange because I don't
even notice June bugs anymore,
not since the times we used to
spend together.

SEPTEMBER NIGHTS

I miss those
September nights.
Being soft,
floating
between your smile
and the things
I can't explain,
like how some things end
before they ever begin,
or how something
so beautiful
can be so destructive.
I've looked love
straight in the eyes,
the sweetest heartache,
dressed in white.
I've rearranged my brain
just to wrap my heart around it
and somehow,
I still find myself
bound to you
in the softness of those
September nights.

I thought we'd make it,
I really did.
But fate had other plans for us
in the end.

ETERNAL SOMEDAY

We were haunted by hope
and paralyzed by fear,
as we stood on the edge
waiting for someday.

Someday is the place
at which we never arrive,
and the place we never leave.

It keeps hope alive.

It is *what if*
on a continuous loop,
a safe distance for fools
and their fearful hearts.

It is forever
just as it is never,
and it is filled with hope
and nothing more.

YOU

You are the butterflies
and the regret,
you are the face
I'll never forget.

You are the raging storm
under my skin,
the tears of the sky,
the downpour within.

You are sweet Sunday smile,
the knock at the door,
the beautiful stranger,
the rose and the thorn.

You are the ghost in the hall,
and the fire in my heart,
the magic, the misery,
the silent alarm.

THAT SONG

You were that song
on the radio
I hadn't heard in a long time.
The one I always seemed
to catch the tail end of,
and even though
I didn't know all the words,
I would sing my heart out.
But it was always over
too soon.

And some days my heart
still plays a song
that sounds a lot like
the way we used to be.

MAGIC

We were some kind
of magic.
We were also a series
of bad decisions,
wrong turns,
and misunderstandings.
But I will never forget
the magic.

WHAT LEAVES

Mother warned me
to never hold tight
to what tries to leave.
Said I might not like
what stays behind,
said it was how
ghosts are made.

THE OLD YOU

I held on
a little longer
than I should have
because I thought
the old you
might come back.

SPACE

I don't know what to say to you,
it's just all gone. Vanished
into thin air, erased,
never there.

And now I have all this space.

WHITE FLAGS

We dwindle away
to a see-through state
with our icebox hearts
and broken dreams.
We wave white flags
with our painted smiles
and pantomime eyes.
We scream into the void
and hope for the best.

SAFE

We could be anything,
yet we choose
to remain strangers,
desperate for the danger
that we will always deny
because we would
rather feel safe
than take the risk.
Instead of living,
we just exist.

THE DISTANCE

The wind blows
down to bones, cold.
Goodbye never sleeps
or leaves my lips,
but in my mind,
it's been said
a thousand times.
We can only be
flightless little birds
for so long, singing
songs of yesterday
before distance
closes in.

STRANGERS AGAIN

Here we are,
strangers again.
Our souls
stopped talking
and somewhere
along the way
our hearts wandered
down the hall.

HEART IN A BOX

She didn't want
anything black
on Sunday,
so, she put her
heart in a box
and she saved it
for someday.

FADE

They don't always fade away.
Sometimes, they grab
a hold of your soul
and never leave.

BUT DARLING YOU ARE FADING

Throw back the last of memories,
drain the well dry.
Get drunk on the spirits,
weep for the wreckage,
bleed bright red nostalgia onto paper
until the last drop of hope spills out.

This is where I let the ghosts let me go.

Start at the ache where the soul is sick
it sings with grief. As we were,
is no longer, I am what remains;
a raven-haired exorcist, I owe you
no ordinary death.

This is where I pull you from my bones.

Extricate myself from this old love
that knows my name and leaves
my late-night calls buried in my throat.
Tear your hooks from my heart,
turn myself inside out.
Face the wound toward the sun.

This is where I burn you out of my soul.

Clear out every hidden compartment
that I ever had you stashed away in.
Wipe down the walls, wash every
surface clean until nothing is you
and everything is new.

This is where I leave the grave.

I never wanted to forget your face,
but darling, you are fading.

SO CLOSE

Don't stand so close
to the ghosts.
Some will haunt you,
and even worse,
some will give you hope.

STRANGERS

In the beginning
we are strangers
and sometimes
in the end
we are even less.

IT COMES BACK

It comes back, it always comes back.
The things you didn't deal with, the feelings
you didn't sort out. You can go years and years
without thinking about it, and then one day,
out of the blue, it taps you on the shoulder
and says, *Oh hey, remember me?*

STILL HAUNTED

I know that they
still haunt you,
I know you're in
soul deep.
There is something
very telling
about the ghosts
we choose to keep.

ECHOES

Sometimes
after nightfall,
when the wind
is soundless,
I secretly wish
that even the echoes
will forget your name.

THE MIDNIGHT HOUSE

The night fades into me
or perhaps it's the other way around,
but it makes no difference because

I always end up here,
on the other side of sunshine
between the hush of four walls
with scorched palms
and black feathers
in clenched fists.

I always end up here,
in the red room
with amber glow and body dust
where the nightmare never screams
and the worry whispers terror so loud
it makes the morning seem so far away.

I always end up here,
with nostrils caked in soot and ash
where it stinks of singed hair and burnt skin
folding in on memories
where the door is ajar
and my eyes are glued shut.

The things that wander in.

STRANGLEHOLD

The way your own heart betrays you.
The way it holds out hope for ghosts.
The way it latches on to what is gone.
The way it refuses to let go.

When it leaves behind its corpse,
do not resuscitate.
But if you're like me,
you will try many times.

IN THE COMPANY OF GHOSTS

They say goodbye
but then you find yourself
keeping company with
the ghosts they leave behind.

THE PAST

Sometimes
we make a home
of the past,
waiting
for the ones
who are never
coming back.

UNFASTENED

I climb out of myself,
my delicate spirit comes loose.
Is this the way to heaven?

I walk across dampened earth,
unfastened and free.
Worms writhe beneath my feet.

Take us too,
a pile of bones beckons.

I turn before the frenzy comes.
I leave before it shows its teeth.
The woods are still on my skin.

I pass four horses and a cemetery,
I think I might be sad forever.
I drip with sleep.

I DON'T WANT TO BE A SAD GHOST

My heartache only sings
in the middle.
I don't want to be a sad ghost.

I don't want to start like a memory
and forget how to leave.
I don't want to be the recurring dream
playing for an empty room.

I don't want to be the hunger behind eyelids,
so weightless and patient.
I don't want to be the spirit hanging
on the owl light.

My heartache only sings
in the middle.
I don't want to be a sad ghost.

THE GIRL WITH CACTUS EYES

There once was a girl
with cactus eyes
and no matter how she tried
she just could not cry.
So, she went into town
with her mason jar,
and collected all the tears
from the broken hearts.

REMAINS

You can bury it,
but one day
it's either going to
claw its way out
from the grave
or you'll end up
exhuming its remains.

PART II

May we find
peace in the pieces
when we must
come undone

THE KITCHEN

When I was five years old,
we moved into a house
where the previous owner
died in the kitchen.

I didn't learn of this until years later.

I used to wake
in the middle of the night
and wander into the hallway,
and from several feet away,
I would just stare into the kitchen.

I would always see something
that appeared to be floating
just below the chandelier.
It was paralyzing.

To me, as a child,
it looked something like
a plastic bag,
or a bubble,
or a jellyfish.
Not see-through,
but like frosted glass.
It was frightening.

Once able to move,
I would make my way
to my parent's room
and stand outside their door,
frozen;

and I would whimper
into the crack of the door
until they would wake
and take me to bed.

LIKE JELLYFISH

Some ghosts are like jellyfish,
swimming through the air
· as if they were never human.

So strange and translucent,
freefalling for small moments.
Wavering in spaces between
then and now. Catching

glimpses of half-eaten dreams
with their twenty-four eyes,
hovering over the ocean floor
with no brain or heart.

Sucked into the earth
and transformed
into memories floating footless
in your house.

GLIMMER

There is something
in the way that you haunt me,
a glimmer of hope, maybe.

The way you show up in dreams
and bleed into reality,
as if you never left.

And I suppose
I've taken comfort
in the company of your ghost.

I IMAGINE

I imagine if you left
I'd bury my aching bones
in the yard
behind the old shed
in the lonely garden
and I'd let the worms
and the dirt
take care of the rest.

I imagine after some regret
I'd dig them up
and they'd sprout faces
of strangers who'd
promised me daisies.

And these bones of mine,
I imagine,
would ache much less.

WAKE THE SPIRITS

Won't you meet me in the after,
where I remain and you are gone?
Where there are no angels, devils,
or ghosts, but an empty house—
won't you come?

Won't you meet me in the void,
where my heart betrays me
and hope survives?
Where the earth is frozen
and the sky is white—
won't you come?

Won't you whirl your wind around me
or place a whisper on my pillow?
Won't you leave a song outside my door
to break the silence in this house?

Won't you meet me in the winter,
when it's midnight and turned cold?
When I've outgrown the void
and outlived the hope,
when my soul believes you're gone?

Won't you meet me by the old maple,
where you left me when we were young?
We'll tell stories and wake the spirits:
I want to know what you've been up to—
won't you come?

WHISPER

I whisper your name to the wind.
Let it carry you over,
till we meet again.

TELL ME

Sit with me, tell me everything.
I stay up every night waiting for a sign—
did you make it to the other side?
Tell me, have you touched the stars
since you went away?
And will I be able to find you
when it's my turn to leave this place?

RETURN

I wonder if you'll return
if I wait for you
under the winter moon
just before the night slips away
I wonder if you'll return?

SOULMATES

Some soulmates can't stay,
but they leave a mark
on your heart
that can't ever be erased.

I WAIT

I go up to the attic
and light some candles.
I put on Pink Floyd's
Wish You Were Here
try to summon your ghost
but you don't come.

I wait for you
in the frigid room
of this vacant house
where windows rumble
with rattleboned hope.

At midnight calm
when day is undone
I talk into the dark
counting spirit orbs
but you never come.

At forest's edge
whispering wishes
when the birds have flown
nine, ten, eleven
I wait for you.

THE WIND

When we finally
make our way
out of this mess,
this flesh,
bare boned
and boundless,
with nothing
but the wind
wrapped around
our souls—
I hope our paths cross
in the northern air,
with our hearts
dipped in sunshine
and whole again.

NOT GOODBYE

And I will find you
in every sunrise by the lake
in every morning coffee
in every whisper on the wind.

And I will love you
to the ends of the earth
in every space and time
in every shadow and dream.

And I will carry you
in every moment
in every atom of my being
beyond infinity.

And I will not say goodbye
for this is not the end
this magic will never die
this love will live on.

Oh, lover of mine,
my heart holds you close
and my soul forever
dances with yours.

FATE

And if one day
fate shows up at my door,
I hope it brings you too.

HOME

Most days
I still look for you
as if I'm trying
to find my way
home.

OLD COAT

Tiny leaves fall and land
on the lapel of my old wool coat
that should have been laid to rest
long ago.

It is worn, but warm,
and it will live to see
another winter.

I pair it with my favourite scarf
that reminds me of the tartan tam
papa used to wear.

The secret pocket jingles,
I pull out a dime
and smile.

SHOEBOX

Old letters and photographs
in a shoebox
under the bed.
Hello.

I spend the afternoon
shuffling through
faded faces
and weathered pages.

I bring you back again.

Time gets away from me,
it always does.
It's so easy to get lost
in old love letters, cards,
and ticket stubs from all
the concerts we loved.

Suddenly I hear the little feet
scampering across the
kitchen floor,
it's already four o'clock.
Mommy, Mommy, where are you?
We're home!

At any moment, the babes
will come crashing through
the bedroom door.

Time to put the memories away,
pack them back into the shoebox
and slide it under the bed.

Goodbye.

I bury you again.

CAUGHT

I caught myself
thinking about you,
the way that I used to.
It was fleeting,
but for that moment,
you were here with me
again.

HIDING PLACE

A ghost once told me
that the best place to hide
is in the depths
of a hopeful mind.

THE NOISE

Some days
the noise
is softer than
the silence,
and kinder than
the quiet
that still listens
for your voice.

BLURRED LINES

How easily
we blur the lines
between memories
and the ghosts.

THE VISIT

Feathers and butterflies,
flickering lights and coins…
I knew these were all from you.

I have dimes stashed away in my pockets.
They're collecting on countertops,
ledges, and bookshelves.
You've been visiting a lot.

I've heard if the dead
should ever come to you in a dream,
that you shouldn't leave with them.
If they extend their hand
and try to lead you away,
you shouldn't go.
But in this dream,
we're already walking arm in arm
towards the sunset.

Your eyes are the same as I remember,
but you look older in death than I recall
in life. I can't smell you or hear you.
It's like a silent movie
that I'm simultaneously watching
and starring in.

There is a persistent ache, a gnawing wish
to rewind, to return to old times.
But we are not walking in that direction.
I don't even question where we are going,
where you are taking me.

We are walking towards water.

Maybe we are going to the beach.
I see the sun in your eyes.

It is so still and quiet.
There are cars and buildings, not people.
There is just the two of us.
This place is familiar,
yet I have never been here before.
You smile at me.

It's you and it's not you.
You're different.
Your mannerisms aren't quite the same.
You're with me, but you're not.
You're like a hologram,
I reach for you,
but I can't grasp you.
It feels cruel.

I miss your softness and quirks.
Your comfort.
I'm homesick again.
We never reach the water,
the beach
or wherever it is that we were going.
But I haven't stopped feeling you since.

THE CALL

Mom called me, upset, and crying.
She said she got a call from dad,
but that's impossible. He's gone.

She told me it was his voice
on the other end. He said he doesn't
like it there and he wants to come home.
She hung up the phone in fear.

I wish I had been there.
I would have talked to him.
I really wanted to talk to him.

A few days later, I'm visiting mom
and just as I'm about to leave,
the phone rings.

I answer, not thinking much of it:

Hello.
I don't like it here.
I want to come back.

Dad… it was dad.

He sounded so far away and the connection
wasn't good. But there was no mistaking
the very distinctive rasp in his voice.

I snapped in fear and hung up.
He never called again.

WINTER

What if I outlive them all
and I am left here all alone?
Who will bury these wretched
bones, when Winter comes
to take me home?

PAPER DOLLS

When I was eight years old,
I saw a floating lady in our little house
on Beechwood Avenue.
Mom and dad turned the front room
into their bedroom and installed
a bifold door for privacy.

One night, while dad was in the hospital
for some minor surgery,
I got to sleep in the bed with mom.
I woke up in the middle of the night
and glanced at dad's picture on the wall.
He looked so handsome in uniform.
Dad was in the British Armed Forces
during WWII and stationed in South Africa.

I heard something at the front door.
There was clanging, as if someone
was carrying something made of metal.
Too afraid to move,
I tried nudging mom awake,
but she was sound asleep.

I heard it again, it was closer.
The bifold door rattled,
and a tall woman entered the room.
She was dressed in a dark hooded robe,
I couldn't see her face.
She was not walking, but floating,
and she was carrying something noisy.

She stopped at the foot of the bed
and looked up at dad's picture.

She didn't even acknowledge me.
I was terrified,
but she never once looked at me.
I think I was invisible to her.

She just kept staring at dad
for quite some time.
Then she turned and floated
right through the bifold door,
disappearing into the night,
never to return.

I told mom about it in the morning,
she said I was just dreaming.
Later in the day, she took me out
and bought me some paper dolls
to make me feel better.

But I never forgot about the floating lady.
She never left my memory.

ACROSS MY HEART

They come and go
across my heart,
when the wind raps
on my window,
when the day
has slipped away.
When the darkness
arrives before dinner
in the early days
of December,
they come and go
across my heart.

GHOST STORY

I thought I saw you
out of the corner of my eye,
but it was just your ghost
playing tricks on my mind.

Your ghost lives
in my peripheral vision.
It whispers in my ear,
I'm still here.

It speaks to me
through muffled voices
in crowded places,
in and around
the everyday shuffling.

It makes contact through
the eyes of countless strangers,
who I don't really think know
what it is to be haunted or surely,
they would turn away and
spare me your gaze.

OBLITERATE ME

To the night I say:
Obliterate me.
Let this quiet brutality
save me.

I undo myself here,
at the edge of my being;
like a hovering apparition,
a dweller.

I come because
the woman in the wall
is whispering again:

The longer you stay
The stronger the cage

I come for the ones
who brought me here,
the ones who came
before me.

With little horrors
embedded in my bones,
I come to break chains,
to part ways
with patterns and pain.

I come to sit with
the worn and wise ones,
long-lost, but certain there is more.

I come here to shatter,
to free shadows,
to breathe.

MESS

Piece by piece,
I will put myself back together
and make something beautiful.
But first, this is the mess I must make.

UNINVITED

The darkness
comes uninvited
and wraps itself
around my bones.
Sometimes they scream,
but they do not break.

NOT THE END

When these
fragile bones
wash ashore
and find you
piled up
and broken,
lifeless,
but not dead,
I want you to know:
this is not the end.

BENEATH THE SURFACE

And sometimes
we fall apart
in the quietest way—
beneath the surface
of calm seas,
we go to battle,
but we don't make
any waves.

THE ROAD

And maybe we aren't lost,
maybe this is just the way.

Here I dwell, at the bottom,
among hard goodbyes
and bittersweet endings,
where there is no end in sight—
Just a road, a lonely road,
that leads to anywhere
I want to go.

THE TRAVELLER

When I was a traveller, I made my way
to anywhere but here.
I was met by malignant spirits,
their killing hum hanging thick on the night air,
and devils with sad eyes
who never really cried any real tears.

"There are no angels here," they laughed.

So, I tucked hell in my pocket
and trudged through grey space
and displaced grief,
beyond the mirrors and the microscopes,
far away from myself.
I made my way past the spirits and the devils,
and I entered the darkness to seek the truth.

I am the storm approaching.
I can take it all back.

RAVEN SONG

She sings with the ravens,
they dance upon her heart.
Feathers fall like fortunes
and bring her comfort
in the dark.

SKELETONS

You can dismantle
those skeletons
all you want,
but someday
those bones
are going to talk.

THE GIRL AND THE MONSTER

Some days
I'm more girl
than monster.
Some days
I wonder what
the monster
has done with
the girl.

SCARS

They ask me why
I shine so bright:
this is what happens
when scars turn to light.

.

PART III

Within the wreckage
is the promise,
of a new beginning

Hungry For Ghosts

WALK-IN CLOSET

And one day
her skeletons
began to suffer
from claustrophobia,
so, she built them
a walk-in closet
where they lived
happily ever after.

POUR

I am full
to the brim,
dragging
the years behind
through
the years ahead.
I am overflowing,
gushing
over my edges,
spilling
across the table,
dripping
onto the floor.
I am pouring
into
a puddle,
a lake,
an ocean;
accumulating
on the surface,
a waterbody
at war.

HEAVY THINGS

I carry them
in thorns
and flowers,
in pounds
and regret.

I carry them
in blood
and dollars,
in this life
and the next.

I carry them
in hopes
and dreams,
in maybes
and what ifs.

These heavy things,
they aren't everything.
But I carry them.

I WONDER

I get to thinking about
how long I have carried
certain things around with me.

Things I am not sure
I will ever unload.
Things buried so deep
they are embedded in my soul,
and perhaps beyond my reach.

Is it even baggage anymore,
or has it broken down
and been absorbed?
Is it in my blood and bones?

I wonder.

WHEN I'M READY

Maybe I'm carrying
the weight
a little bit longer,
but I'm building muscle
and I'm getting stronger.
Slow and steady,
the healing comes.
I'll move on
when I'm ready,
I'll let go
on my own terms.

EXIST

I have this fear that my existence
will land somewhere between
not quite alive and not quite dead.

That I will be too light to sink,
too heavy to soar,
that I will just linger in the middle;
hover and teeter.

That I will drift with the winds
of common days and call it living,
merely picking out the good bits
from the dust and debris.

That long after the love song stops playing,
my heart will still hope, still wish, still stay.
That I will have to hit the bottom
if I'm ever to begin again.

SONG OF FLAMES

They tell you to follow the sun
as if night isn't upon you,
as if the shadows aren't real.
But night is still upon you.

The thing in your mouth, copper hush.
Rage whispers and silence screams until
you sing your song of flames:

Let them come, let them rage
Let them find me in the shadows
Let them say my name and quake.

They tell you to let go
as if you've unpacked your pain,
as if you've poured it into the earth.
But Hell still sits in a suitcase.

The thing in your belly, it knows.
The magic lies in the coming apart,
in the middle of the wreck,
in your every season and every room,
it waits.

Hurt is hard to feel,
But still the wound must speak
And speak it does before you heal.

They tell you to sit on the moon,
to keep fishing dark skies for stars
as if hope isn't hanging by a thread of nostalgia,

as if you didn't notice the rage behind the flowers
before they were plucked from your garden.
But his hands are still entangled in your hair.

The thing in your centre, it calls.
Little by little, in waves,
it comes.

Pull up a chair, sorrow says
Out of body, slip.
You will rebuild yourself
But first, rest.

I JUST AM

I am not where I was
or where I am headed.
I am here, in-between,
living the moment;
sometimes with certainty,
sometimes on a whim.
I am neither lost nor found
I just am.

HEART RULES

Ruled
by the heart
I have suffered,
but oh
how I have
conquered.

WARRIOR

Here I stand, a wreck
in the wreckage,
but this is not the end.
I am a warrior,
I build myself from the ground up:
this is where I begin again.

PIECES (THREE DIFFERENT ONES)

I

I want to say
that you took
pieces of me,
I really do,
but the truth is,
I gave them to you.
Maybe you needed them
more than I did,
and that's okay.
I'm not crumbling,
I'm still standing,
I'm okay,
and I hope you are too.

II

Keep the pieces
you took from me.
I can't put them back,
I've outgrown them,
they won't fit.

III

One day I just woke up
and realized
that I had become
a stranger to myself,
and all my pieces
were being held together
by all the things
I appeared to be.

LOVE STILL FINDS ME

I am nowhere and love still finds me.
On feather toes
and gentle wind,
it drops in.

It settles in the hollow,
drowning out the echoes.
Some of the echoes say your name.
Some float away.

I wait outside the seawall,
untangled and unshackled.
I hold no phantoms hostage,
swim away, swim away.

I am nowhere and love still finds me.
On feather toes
and gentle wind,
it pulls me from the wreck.

I AM EXTRAORDINARY

I am extraordinary.
I am a wreck
and a masterpiece,
in equal parts.
I am a warrior,
I will get through,
no matter what it takes.
It won't be easy,
but I am determined
and unstoppable.
I will overcome
and rebuild.
I will bloom from the decay,
and I will thrive.
I will burn, break, and bleed.
I will wear my scars proud,
and I will rise from the ruins—
not unscathed,
but free.

THE LEAF

The leaf hangs on
to a branch of a tree.
It's the only one left
that has yet to fall away.
It waits for the wind
to help it break free.
I sit and observe:
Hey, that's me.

UNRAVEL

Sometimes it's in
the downward spiral
of coming undone,
where we truly begin to see
who we really are.
The more we unravel,
the closer we get
to being free.

UNDONE

This is where
I come undone
and put myself
back together—
not like before,
but better.

THE DANCE

The darkness wanted to
dance with me, so, we danced.
Only this time, it was my turn to lead.

UNEARTH

I unearth old versions of me.
I will honour and celebrate them:
The women in the shadows.
The knowing in my bones.
The ghosts of who I used to be.

CHANGING

I am moving parts.
My pieces are continuously
circulating and rearranging.
A new me is taking form:
Underneath this skin,
this human casing,
I am changing.

AMONG THE RUINS

Before I put myself
back together
I spent some time
among the ruins—
a dark and
magnificent place
where I got to know
all the pieces of my soul—
Pieces of me
that I didn't even know existed.

STILL LEARNING

I am still learning
to be gentle with myself
and to give myself grace.
I am still learning
that it's okay to not be okay
and that struggling
doesn't equate to defeat.

DEPTHS

And if I get
swallowed
into the depths
of myself,
may I stay
down there
long enough
to drown
in the truth.

SEEDS

We plant
the seeds
beneath
the bruise.
It hurts
like hell,
but then
we bloom.

THE GARDEN

I buried myself,
not in a graveyard,
but a garden,
beneath frozen ground.
A winter maiden
with scratched earth
under my fingernails
and a blackbird
in my chest,
I fell.

BLOOM

I poured myself
into the earth—
only the flowers
would know my pain.
And I thought,
I might drown,
I might die
a thousand deaths,
before I would ever
bloom again.

But bloom, I did,
again and again.

MORNING SUN

The morning Sun makes her way through my window.
She puts her hands upon my face, *it's time to wake.*
But I don't want to, I tell her I'm not ready. You see,
sleep is my escape. She just shines even brighter,
it's time to seize the day.

HOPE RISES

And just
as the sun rises,
so does the hope
in my heart.

REBUILD

And it's okay,
all this undoing:
I am ready to rebuild.

DISMANTLED

There was something
in the way she dismantled herself,
the way she pulled fire from the sun
and burned.

The way she lay face down
in the rubble, breathing in
ash and despair.

The way she tasted the destruction
before she carved herself anew
from the black sky.

The way she fell motionless
into the arms of grief,
wide open to the night.

The way she surrendered to the collapse
before finding strength
in vulnerability.

The way she embraced midnight
and found herself in the absence
of the sun.

The way she took it all back.
Her happiness
Her freedom
Her life.

RUINS AND ROYALTY

I am not looking
for the person I used to be,
she's gone.
But I am on my way,
and I am bringing
fire and purpose,
and when I arrive,
they will all know:
I am ruins,
I am royalty, so
tell the ghosts I'm home.

THE THING ABOUT HOPE

Hope is heavy at times
and other times,
it becomes your wings
and lifts you up.
That's the thing about hope,
sometimes you carry it
and sometimes it carries you.

THE STORM OF THE BECOMING

This is where the healing begins.
Right here, right now.
Stripped down to skeleton and truth,
naked and aware of the mess and destruction.
This is where you leave yourself.
This is where you return to yourself.
This is the storm of the becoming.

When you are someone else
on the outside looking in,
a stranger in your own skin,
this is the skin you must shed.

When the weeds run rampant,
when you stop pruning
and watering your garden.
When the bloodsuckers come
to feed and feast,
when you give it all away—

Here, take everything.

They will pick and pluck
and it will never be enough.
When there is nothing left,
they will take more
until you are drained dry.

This is where you leave yourself,
that version of you,
to decompose and seep
into the earth.

This is where the healing begins.
Right here, right now.
Stripped down to skeleton and truth,
naked and aware of the mess and destruction.
This is where you leave yourself.
This is where you return to yourself.
This is the storm of the becoming.

CAGE

If confinement
ever comes to you
dressed as comfort,
may you
have the strength
to acknowledge it
and the courage
to break free.
May you
never have to
live your life
inside a cage.

AT THE SEABED

I dumped my bones in the ocean,
watched them sink to the bottom
and wondered, what might come back up.
Would it be a different person?
Something else?

I dwelled in the depths of those dark waters
neither coming up for air nor drowning
and took a place at the seabed
with my past selves.

The strange and mysterious ones,
the knowing in my bones who had been here all along.
They are the ones from before and the ones to come,
and in the middle of a great big mess,
their whispers turned to roars—

Sometimes new beginnings start at the bottom.

How freeing it is,
to have this weight lifted
and these chains broken,
to miss the wreckage
a little less.

GARDENS from GRAVES

The forthcoming poetry collection from

KRISTIN KORY

AVAILABLE SPRING 2024

Gardens From Graves

FETCHING SEEDS

If you ask me about being strong
or resilient
or brave

I'll tell you about unfolding edges
and rebuilding
from a million little pieces
despite the wreck that remains

and digging the dirt
to bedrock
to fracture and shatter
splinter and break.

I'll tell you about going downward
and inward
and meeting with sorrow
and speaking to pain

and when hell spills from your bones
that you'll fetch seeds
from the dried-up darkness
and grow gardens from graves.

HEART AND BONE

When I wash ashore
hollow like a seashell
still and alone

rest your ear upon my soul
and listen to the echoes
of heart and bone

telling you
we are never empty
or very far from home.

LULLABY WAVES

Hope sails in on a lilac breeze.

It's last dream standing
the fountainhead of undying wishes
that makes a body soft enough to fall
and it might leave you in limbo
might leave you cold

until it hits you
between sky and earth
midstorm
where your heart is a bottomless pit
and hunger demands death

to the fading pseudo sun
and withering strands of gold
that fasten you to fancy.

It touches down on tippy-toes
wistful winds churn ocean in
lullaby waves—

a hymn for wrecked hearts
who've given up their ghosts
and for the doomed dreamers
who keep them close.

Hope sails in on a lilac breeze
and then it leaves.

THE CORPSE AT THE DOOR

If you ask me about hope
I'll tell you about the days
when it knocks on my door
and I don't answer.

When it comes to soften edges
and feed phantoms
when it's the cruel caller, the corpse at the door
when it waits dead.

On those days
I don't want what it brings
so I become the wind
and I declare the storm.

I don't want what it brings
so I tear the roof from this house
and the sky falls in.

Old wounds shake loose.

JUST A DEATH AND A WINDING ROAD

First exit at the roundabout
straight ahead
turn right at the crossroads
go through the tunnel
and then it's just a death and a winding road left to go.

I made it to the lake by light
and waited
for the wind to pick up waves
to crash on rocks
to blow through trees

and the clouds couldn't tell if I said your name that day.

IF ONLY

If only we could go back
to summer afternoons
on the deck
in camping chairs
feet upon the railing
smoking cigarettes
and pinners
that sometimes led to
midnight steaks.

To autumn evenings
on Lakeshore
in the red Ford
driving by, not stalking
the odd silver fox
and coffee
and the best talks
in parking lots.

To winter nights
and endlessness
on the deck
freezing our asses off
smoking cigarettes
and pinners
in camping chairs
before you went north
if only.

WE'RE NOT ALL BLESSED WITH EXIT WOUNDS

If you ask me about letting go
I'll tell you that we're not all blessed
with exit wounds
and it doesn't always leave your body—
sometimes it's the thing you carry.

I'll tell you that one day you'll turn it loose
you'll let it go away from you
but some things aren't so easily
scattered to sea—
sometimes it's easier to let it stay

until the sun that comes from nowhere
cuts holes in the darkness
and breaks you open

and when it pulls misery from night
and burdens from body
I'll tell you that you'll find feathers
in the spaces left behind.

NOT A GRAVEYARD

Sometimes wounds weep hunger
and build houses for the dead
and sometimes you forget
where you are—

waiting in line for a scar
for hope to fall from the bone
and it never comes easy
when you still got those dirty love songs in your head

and when it comes crawling back
you forget who you are
and the past is a stranger you wake to
nuzzling into the blank of your warm body
snug as a bug in your bed.

Sometimes you forget
and you swear you're not a graveyard
not a house for the dead.

IN THE WIND

Sitting in the kitchen
I stare at her—
I can't believe how fast
she is growing up.

A cool breeze blows in
through the patio window
and she says,
I wish I lived in the wind.

GLIMPSE

In our silences
where we feel most safe
we catch a glimpse

of us
at the threshold
passing through

we wonder at our blessings—
second glances and
second chances

we are learning to trust our hearts again.

CATCHING SNOWFLAKES

Catching snowflakes
how gracefully they fall
and when they touch down
it doesn't hurt at all.

LOVE POEMS

Sometimes I write love poems
on the backs of old work papers
arranging words carefully
sometimes recklessly
and they always sound like you
when I read them out loud.

ABOUT THE AUTHOR

Kristin Kory is a Canadian poet and author, who discovered her passion for writing as a teenager growing up in Hamilton, Ontario.

She is inspired by nature, music, and the unknown, and draws inspiration from both light and darkness. Her words are equal parts inspiring, empowering, and haunting. Her poetry and prose range from love and heartbreak, to healing, self-love, and growth.

In addition to Hungry for Ghosts, she has been published in anthologies from 300 South Media Group, and Augie's Bookshelf Publishing Company.

Kristin is a bit of an introvert who loves coffee, thunderstorms, and visiting haunted places.

Follow Kristin Kory

Facebook - KristinKoryAuthor
Instagram – KristinKory_
On the web – kristinkory.com

ACKNOWLEDGMENTS

To my publisher, Jay. Thank you for bringing this book home.

To Candice, Thank you for your kindness and support. I learned so much from you while working together on the first edition. You are incredible.

To Mary Ellen, my kindred spirit, for believing in me, and for your encouragement and support through all the years. To the moon and back, always.

To Eryn, for always being there and cheering me on, and for sharing your strength during your own struggles. You are a warrior. I love you.

To Gerry, for all the songs, laughs, and killer taxi rides; for the unspoken things our hearts will always understand.

To Colleen, for your light and wisdom. Here's to excited felines and cursed Ouija Boards.

To Jason and Michelle, for your unwavering friendship. Real connections never die.

To Avant, for pushing me when I needed it and for your inspiration. For bringing it down to a slow simmer, but most of all, thank you for your friendship. You are stuck with me.

To Georgie, wherever you are. I have never stopped thinking about you.

To my family, for your continuous love and support. You are my world.

To my readers, I am so grateful for your endless support over the years. Thank you for joining me on this journey.

Thank you, heartache.
Thank you, failure.
Thank you, darkness.

I am just getting started.

Made in the USA
Middletown, DE
31 August 2023